C000117619

Not you

...again!

Helping Children Improve Playtime and Lunch-time Behaviour

A Lucky Duck Book

Not you ...again!

Helping Children Improve Playtime and Lunch-time Behaviour

Second Edition

Fiona Wallace
Diane Caesar

P·C·P
Paul Chapman
Publishing

© Fiona Wallace and Diane Caesar 2007

This second edition first published 2007

Apart from any fair dealing for the purposes of research or private study, or criticism or review, as permitted under the Copyright, Designs and Patents Act, 1988, this publication may be reproduced, stored or transmitted in any form, or by any means, only with the prior permission in writing of the publishers, or in the case of reprographic reproduction, in accordance with the terms of licences issued by the Copyright Licensing Agency. Enquiries concerning reproduction outside those terms should be sent to the publishers.

Rights to copy pages marked as worksheets, certificates or overhead foils are extended to the purchaser of the publication for his/her use.

The right of the author to be identified as Author of this work has been asserted by him/her in accordance with the Copyright, Design and Patents Act 1988.

Paul Chapman Publishing
A SAGE Publications Company
1 Oliver's Yard
55 City Road
London EC1Y 1SP

SAGE Publications Inc.
2455 Teller Road
Thousand Oaks, California 91320

SAGE Publications India Pvt Ltd
B 1/I 1 Mohan Cooperative Industrial Area
Mathura Road, New Delhi 110 044

SAGE Publications Asia-Pacific Pte Ltd
33 Pekin Street #02-01
Far East Square
Singapore 048763

www.luckyduck.co.uk

Illustrator: Philippa Drakeford
Activity sheets designed by: Nick Shearn

British Library Cataloguing in Publication data

A catalogue record for this book is available from the British Library

ISBN 978-1-4129-2896-0

Library of Congress Control Number: 2006932495

Typeset by C&M Digitals (P) Ltd, Chennai, India
Printed in India by Replika Pvt, Ltd.
Printed on paper from sustainable resources

A big thank you to
Ben, Jenny, Jerry, Joe, Pete, Rosie and Stephanie our
toughest yet most supportive critics!

Contents

Introduction   viii

About this book   viii

Before you start   ix

Using the worksheets   xii

Further reading and resources   xiv

Session record sheet

The worksheets

Area of difficulty	Worksheet number
Fighting, kicking, pushing	6, 7, 8, 13, 22, 23, 30, 67, 68
Bullying	8, 11, 13, 14, 18, 49, 54, 68, 71, 75
Ball foul play	13, 21, 29
Wet play	77, 78, 79
Cheek, being rude	1, 2, 3, 4, 24, 66, 69, 70
Playing in the toilets	25, 26
Running in and out of school	35, 36, 39
Climbing	32, 33
Dropping litter	15, 16, 19
Inappropriate behaviour in the playground	31, 34, 40, 65, 67, 68, 73
Inappropriate behaviour in the dinner hall	20, 35, 52, 53, 58
Swearing	14, 28, 69, 70
Name calling	9, 10, 14, 28, 42, 60, 72
Spoiling others' games	13, 22, 38, 41, 50
Mistreating others' property	12, 27, 80.
Making things better	5, 42, 60, 63, 64, 66, 69, 70, 71, 72, 73
Being polite	9, 10, 11, 74
Keeping the rules	17, 23, 37, 40, 61, 62

Learning to think   43, 46, 47, 48, 49, 51, 54, 55, 63, 66

Friendships   44, 45, 47, 48, 49, 56, 59, 60, 76

Planning behaviour   50, 51, 53, 57, 58

Blank borders   81

Introduction

About this book

These worksheets and activities have been devised to help teachers, lunchtime supervisors, learning mentors and others who support children in trouble at playtime and lunchtime. They focus on the playground environment and ways to improve behaviour and they link well to the Change for Children agenda as well as the five outcomes in Every Child Matters, 2004. Some of the principles that guided the development of the materials are listed below:

- Staff must be able to deal effectively with a child in trouble without automatically attributing blame to the child or their actions.

- Adults can help children improve their behaviour without resorting to punishment or strategies based on deprivation of pleasurable activities or learning experiences.

- Children should take responsibility for their own actions ... both those that get them into trouble and those that they can take to change their behaviour for the better. The worksheets provide a set of activities that encourage children to think about themselves and their actions in a constructive and critical manner. They provide opportunities to learn new skills that are less likely to get them into trouble.

- No child should be written off as beyond help and neither is any child perfect. There is always the chance to develop or strengthen skills and relationships and improve behaviour.

- Resources for busy staff must be easy to use. These sheets only need copying, which can be done freely within the purchasing establishment. The CD version enables sheets to be tailored to particular situations and put on the purchasing establishment's computer network, thus enabling easy access to the materials by a wide range of staff. The blank borders allow new sheets to be quickly designed to complement the published pack.

The book contains a collection of worksheets that have been designed to address specific problem behaviours that occur in all playgrounds in all educational settings, such as spoiling others' games and poor behaviour in the dinner hall. Other activities are suitable for the child who is often in trouble. These can be personalised so that schools can build up a bank of additional worksheets designed for specific problems or particular individuals.

The materials can be used in any way that suits your particular setting. Staff may choose the sheets most appropriate to each individual child's ability, needs and the problem behaviour to be addressed. Whilst the resources are wide ranging, it is not intended that they will cover every situation that occurs. Other sanctions will still be appropriate and some behaviours will be too serious to be dealt with using these materials without additional measures. It may be relevant to link their usage to a child's individual education or behaviour plan.

Before you start

The procedures agreed for the use of the materials should be discussed and be consistent with behaviour policy, practice and procedures in your setting. You should consider the following questions:

- Who decides to use the materials?
- Who should give out the worksheets?
- Where are they to be done?
- Who will supervise and record their completion?
- What happens to the finished sheet?
- What records are to be kept?
- What future monitoring will be put in place?
- When and how will parents/carers be involved?
- How will new positive behaviours be celebrated?

It is important that all staff have time to debate and agree the above, as consistency is fundamental to effective pupil management. You may find that as a staff group you may not share a common view. However, it is essential that you all work in the same way. In other words *you may not all agree but you must all agree to act in the same way*. You may find the following ideas helpful in exploring views and gaining agreement amongst staff. The reference list gives additional sources of similar activities.

1 Mapping problem behaviour

As a whole group, produce a list of all the problem behaviours that occur in your playground. Divide into smaller groups and work together to place each problem behaviour from your list into one of the four quadrants of the diagram below. Each group should complete their own map:

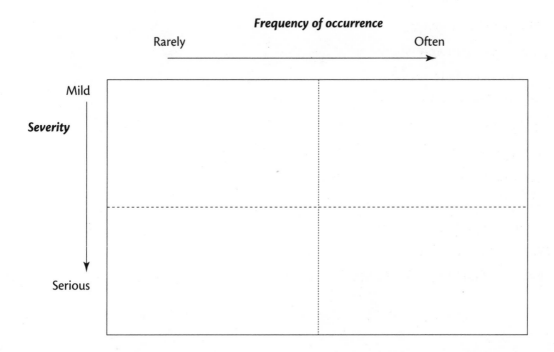

Now work together as a whole group again. Discuss each group's map. Then produce another final map showing your agreed positioning of each problem behaviour. Use this information to select which behaviours to target first.

2   Agreeing strategies

Come up with a list of all the strategies that could be used to deal with difficult behaviour. Agree a coding system and mark each strategy according to:

- how frequently it should be used (sometimes, often, never)
- for which age groups
- by which staff (class teacher, head, lunchtime supervisor, learning mentor, after-school club staff)

Record additional comments at the side of each strategy. Formalise your ideas in writing then distribute copies to all relevant staff with a reminder to stick to the agreements made. Review this from time to time.

3   Seeking pupils' views

Share your list of the most commonly used strategies for handling difficult playground behaviour with groups of pupils or the School Council. Ask the children for their views and whether they consider the strategies would work. Alternatively use your list of problem behaviours and ask the pupils to match appropriate sanctions to behaviours. This is best done in groups rather than individually.

4   Observing playground behaviour

Much information can be generated just by systematically watching what goes on in the playground. Pupils and staff can observe themselves and each other or you may want to ask an outsider, perhaps your school educational psychologist or behaviour support worker. You might look at the following:

- How is the playground used?
- What games are played?
- Who plays them and where?
- Does this create tension?
- What do the staff do?
- Do they interact with the children?
- Where do they stand?
- How many positive comments are made to pupils?
- Are there any patterns to problem behaviour?
- Are there good days and bad days? Why?
- Where and when, exactly, do difficulties occur?
- How is difficult behaviour currently managed?

Make the observations over a reasonable period of time. Gather the information and discuss with pupils and staff to see if changes to current practice are needed and are feasible. Draw up an action plan indicating who will do what, by when. Don't be too ambitious. Start with one thing ... in this way one small change begins to make a difference. Review what you have done and share your successes. Plan new strategies for areas still in need of further development.

How To Use the CD-ROM

The CD-ROM contains a PDF file, labelled 'Worksheets.pdf'. You will need Acrobat Reader version 3 or higher to view and print these resources.

The documents are set up to print to A4 but you can enlarge them to A3 by increasing the output percentage at the point of printing using the page set-up settings for your printer

Using the worksheets

There are 80 photocopiable sheets. Some encourage the child to reflect on the particular behaviour that has got them into trouble, whilst others encourage the child to consider more appropriate behaviour.

Although many children will have been sent in from the playground, completing a worksheet should not be seen as a punishment. The sheets should be enjoyable and a learning opportunity for the child. Children should be given appropriate support to complete them successfully. Working with a child provides an opportunity to discuss the problem behaviour and time out from a difficult situation to calm down. Upset, difficult or angry children are challenging; however, they need your support to complete the task and learn from it.

Children should not be routinely denied all their break time – they need an opportunity to let off steam outside. Each worksheet should occupy a child for no more than 10–15 minutes. For those who work faster, the detailed border may be coloured in to enhance the finished sheet. Only pencils and crayons are needed and most children should be able to work independently, after discussion of the difficulty and a little help to read the worksheet through and get started.

When a child is sent in to complete a sheet they should be quite clear about what they have done wrong. It is helpful to ask the child why they are in trouble so that misunderstandings can be cleared up immediately. A worksheet appropriate to the misdemeanour can then be selected and discussed with the child. Scribing for a child may help them focus on the issue rather than their writing skills.

Once their work is completed, the child should be praised. It is important that staff value the task and the efforts of the child, thereby helping the child remember the message contained in the worksheet. The completed worksheets should be kept as a record of work toward helping a child alter their behaviour. Consider whether the sheets might be shared with parents. The session record sheet on the page following page xiv is designed to help you with this.

The child who is often in trouble

In every school there will be a few children who are frequently in trouble; there is always someone who always seems to be in the wrong place at the wrong time!

The child who is often in trouble may need help to see that there are alternative ways of thinking and behaving which are less likely to get them into trouble. They should learn to think about themselves and be urged to take responsibility for their actions and understand the choices they can make. Children should be encouraged to believe that they can find solutions to their problems. They should be taught that there is always the chance to develop or strengthen relationships with either their peers or the adults they come into contact with. It is likely that other strategies to manage or improve behaviour are already being implemented. Don't forget to link work to the pupil's individual programme; this could include their Individual Education Plan (IEP) or Pastoral Support Plan (PSP). It is always important and useful to liaise with others who work in your setting, as well as parents/carers and other relevant professionals.

There are three types of worksheet in this book:

- Those designed to elicit information about the children, for example their views about themselves, their friendships, likes and dislikes. This information may shed light on some of the factors precipitating difficult behaviour and should assist in planning for change in the child's behaviour.

- Those designed to help the child focus on what he or she actually does at break times and, in particular, what it is that gets him or her into trouble.

- Those designed to promote new skills and more positive attitudes.

It may be helpful if a member of staff works individually with a child who is often in trouble, particularly if he or she is in a younger age group. They should carefully review the completed sheet with them to draw out any information that might be used to help modify behaviour and to develop a positive working relationship. Where problems are common to a group of children the worksheets could be done individually and then discussed in small groups of two or three.

For all children it is particularly important that their work is valued by staff, signed, dated and kept safely. It is important with some of the sheets to respect information the child has given as this may be confidential or could be misinterpreted if it gets out to a wider audience, for example those whom the child dislikes or who get him or her into trouble.

Further reading and resources

There are, of course, numerous resources, both printed and online, addressing problem behaviour in the playground and other settings. A selection of those with very practical advice and suggestions is given below. Unless otherwise mentioned, the publications are available in the *Incentive Plus* catalogue, which is full of posters, games books and other resources (including Lucky Duck books) in the area of behaviour and emotional literacy.

Incentive Plus
6 Fernfield Farm
Little Horwood
Milton Keynes
MK17 0PR

Tel (UK) 01908 526120
www.incentiveplus.co.uk

Active Playtimes is written by Wendy Collin to support playtime supervisors. It focuses on old and new games to help promote positive, active playtimes. The pack contains a booklet and 25 laminated cards giving instructions for games.

Jenny Moseley, well known for her work on circle time, has written *Create Happier Lunchtimes*, guidelines to help midday supervisors deal with all kinds of playtime issues. She has also published, with Georgia Thorp, a practical book called *All Year Round: Exciting Ideas for Peaceful Playtimes*. This accessible and practical book gives a wealth of ideas to create a new framework for playtimes.

In *Celebrations*, a book of photocopiable certificates from George Robinson and Barbara Maines of Lucky Duck, there are enough certificates for every school day of the year, even in a leap year! They cover a wide range of behaviours and personality traits, including many that are not traditionally rewarded. Enjoy browsing the website at www.luckyduck.co.uk.

Those of you who want ideas for staff development activities in the area of behaviour management could get hold of a copy of *100 Activities for Behaviour Management Training Days* by Dave Vizard, the founder of Behaviour Solutions. These activities have been tried and tested in schools across the country and cover issues such as understanding the importance of body language and developing a consistent approach. There is a long list of useful links on Dave's website at www.behaviourmatters.com, from which you can also order his books.

The '*Framework for Intervention*' project, initiated in Birmingham, helps teachers tackle concerns about students' behaviour in schools and nurseries, using school improvement, staff empowerment and environmental change. It works for all ages and in all settings, promoting 'learning behaviour together'. There is also a book particularly focusing on playtimes and lunchtimes, at www.frameworkforintervention.com. Project materials are available through the website or from Incentive Plus.

For those of you who never have time to read anything other than the back of a cereal packet, there is a series of DVDs presented by Bill Rogers covering '*Prevention*', '*Positive Correction*', '*Consequences*' and '*Repair and Rebuild*'. The DVDs are easy to watch and each is about 40 minutes long, presented in a different style. You could dip in and out of them but time taken to view 'Positive Correction' would be time well spent. Watching as a staff group may lead to a valuable discussion about managing behaviour in your setting.

The Primary National Strategy – Excellence and Enjoyment: Social and Emotional Aspects of Learning (DfES 1577 2005 G) is linked to citizenship and focuses on developing children's knowledge, understanding and skills in four key aspects of social and emotional learning: empathy, self-awareness, social skills and motivation. The materials can be freely downloaded from www.standards.dfes. gov.uk.

Session record sheet

Pupil .... Date of session ....

☐ Not You Again!

☐ What Else Can I Do With You?   Worksheet number

☐ Just Stop ... and Think!

Worksheet title...................................Staff initials..

Key points from this session

Actions for staff (What? Who? When?)

Issues for exploration at a future session

Review of progress made in this area   Date ....

'Thank you'

'Thank you' is a polite thing to say in any language.

Colour all the words carefully

Gracias
Spanish

Merci
French

Tak
Danish

Danke
German

Grazie
Italian

Practise saying these to yourself ... then try them on your friends.

Your name _____

Helper's name _____

'Please'

'Please' is a polite thing to say in any language

Colour all the words carefully

Bitte
German

Ludzu
Latvian

S'il vous plait
French

Por favor
Spanish

Practise saying these to yourself ... then try them on your friends.

Your name _____

Helper's name _____

Thank you for saying 'thank you'

No one likes rude people.

Take time to think about saying 'thank you'.

Draw two times when it is important to say 'thank you'.

When do you think people should say thank you to you?

Your name _____   Helper's name _____

Please say 'please'

Saying 'please' can make things happen!

Finish the sentences to make your friends laugh.

You could do them like this:

Please may I have a crocodile for tea?

Please may I have ...

I would like ...   please.

Please could I try ...

No thanks, I would like ...   please.

Please draw pictures to go with your funny sentences.

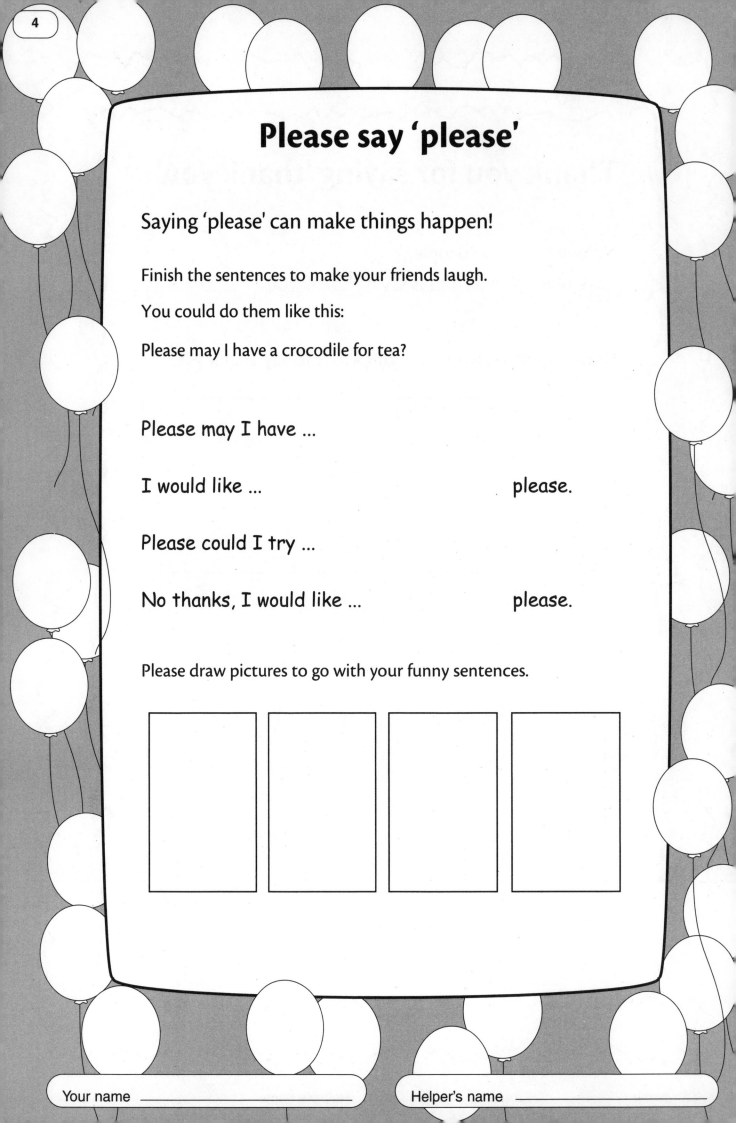

Your name _____   Helper's name _____

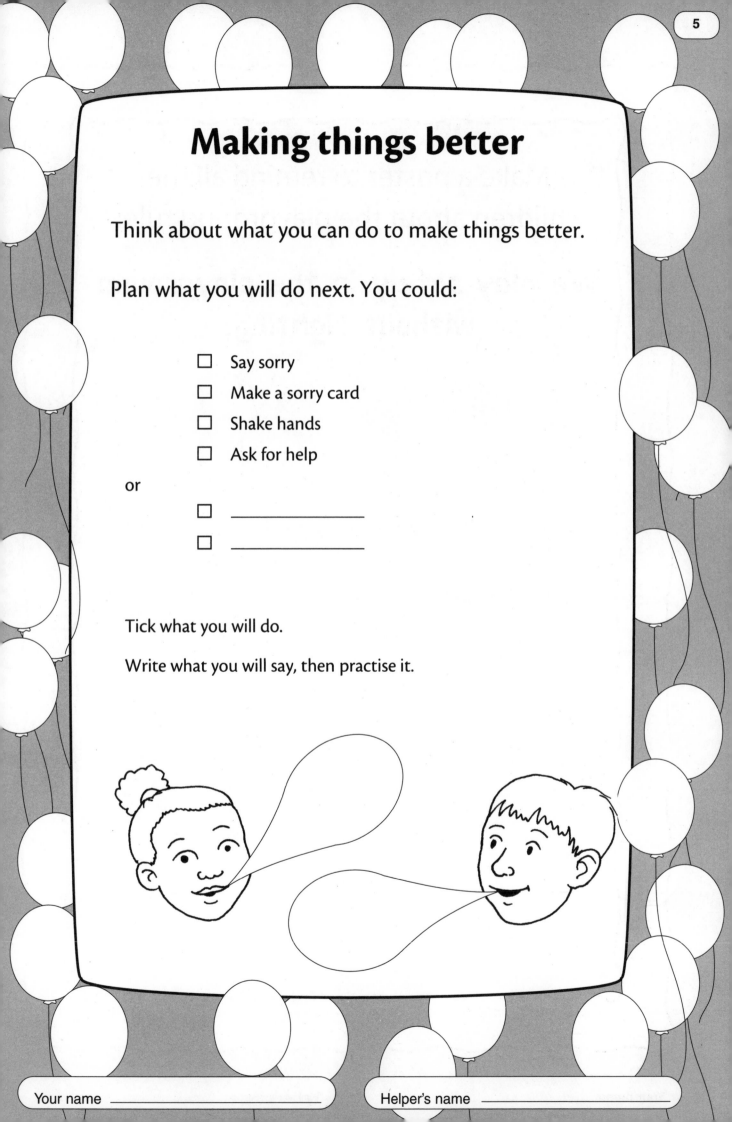

Making things better

Think about what you can do to make things better.

Plan what you will do next. You could:

- ☐ Say sorry
- ☐ Make a sorry card
- ☐ Shake hands
- ☐ Ask for help

or

- ☐ _____
- ☐ _____

Tick what you will do.

Write what you will say, then practise it.

Make a poster to remind all the children about the playground rule:

We play safely in the playground without fighting.

Pushing is dangerous

Do u know how 2 text?

Write a message on this phone screen to a friend to remind them not to push.

Write another to tell them why they should not push.

Make a word search. Put in all these things which you can do in the playground without being told off!

run	skip	smile	laugh
chatter	jump	play	walk
sing	hop	dance	talk

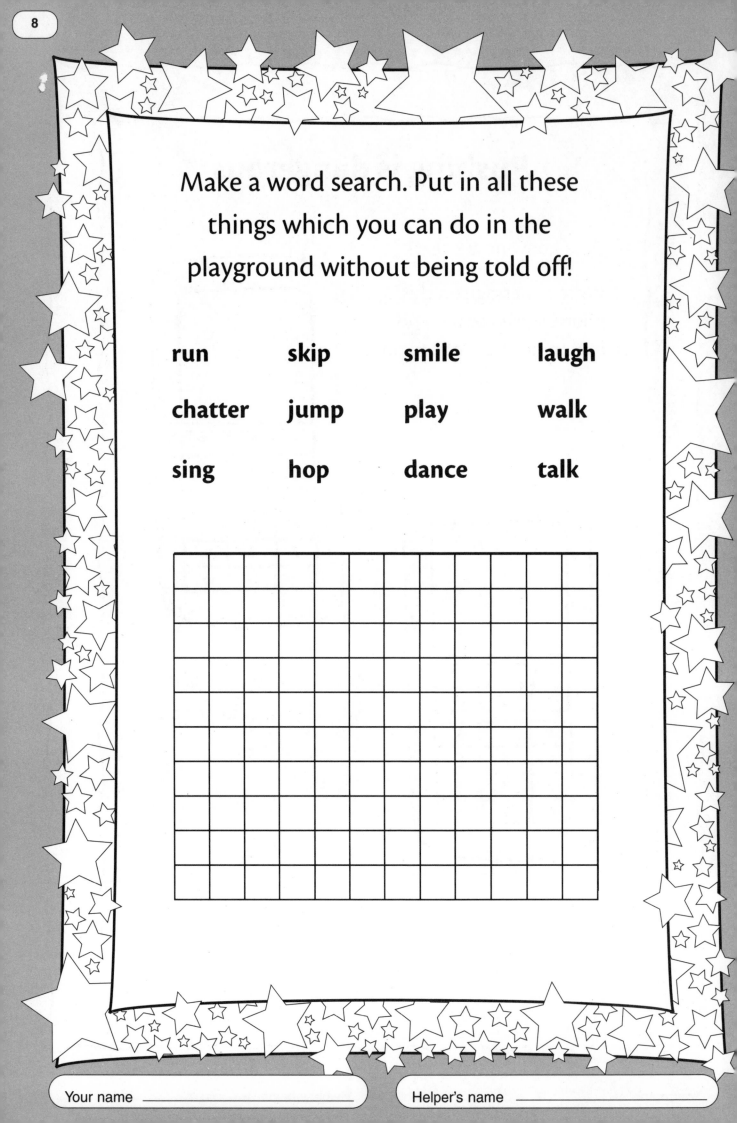

Who helps at playtime?

Finish their faces and write their names.

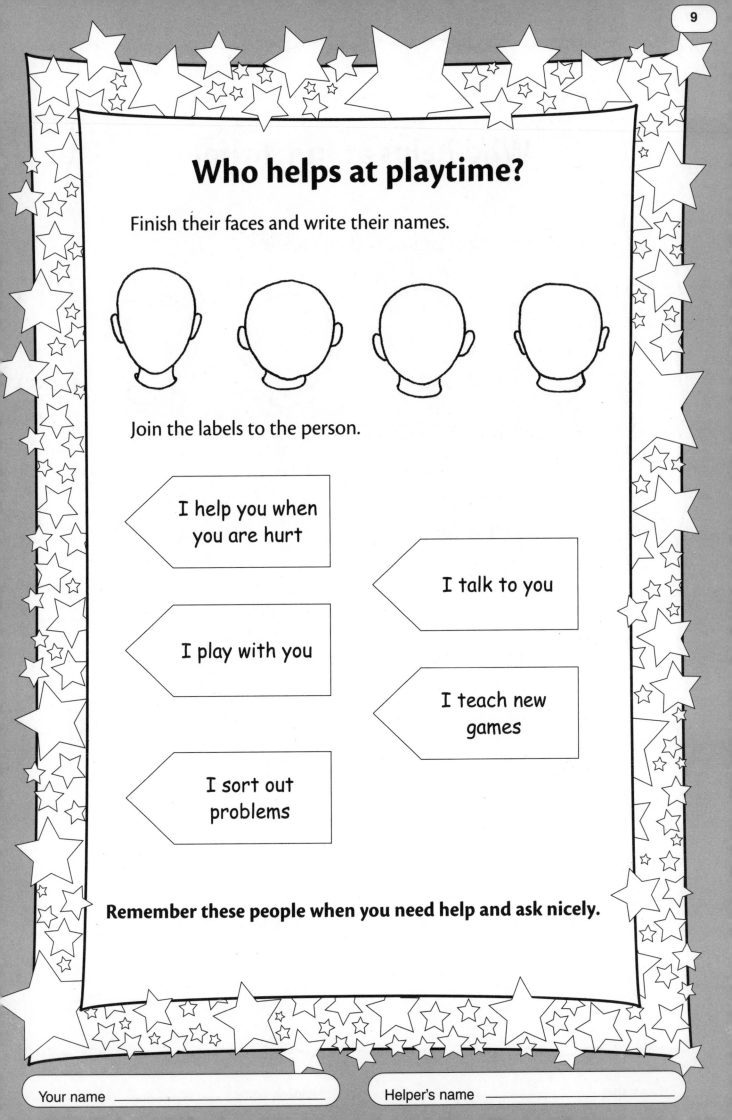

Join the labels to the person.

I help you when you are hurt

I talk to you

I play with you

I teach new games

I sort out problems

Remember these people when you need help and ask nicely.

Your name _____

Helper's name _____

Who helps at lunchtime?

Finish their faces and write their names.

Join the labels to the person.

I cook
the food

I help to
clear up

I give extra help
to some children

I help all
children

I serve the
drinks

I make sure it is
not too noisy

Remember that we help you. Try to be polite to us.

Your name _____

Helper's name _____

Word Search

f	r	i	e	n	d	l	y	a	b	e	s
s	u	o	e	t	r	u	o	c	l	v	t
s	y	z	a	r	q	f	u	t	c	p	h
e	n	x	f	w	d	r	n	c	v	g	o
n	e	e	u	d	q	e	o	p	e	a	u
s	o	w	n	x	g	c	t	n	l	b	g
i	e	t	i	l	o	p	e	m	b	k	h
b	l	g	k	f	y	r	o	z	s	k	t
l	m	o	i	j	o	g	h	t	i	j	f
e	j	o	h	u	i	l	n	n	d	u	u
k	n	d	s	m	g	f	d	h	i	e	l
e	c	i	n	g	c	a	r	e	f	u	l

friendly	thoughtful
kind	generous
polite	fun
gentle	careful
nice	good
sensible	courteous

Your name _____   Helper's name _____

Be honest

Crack the code to discover the message and write it in the box.

A B C D E F G H I J K L M

N O P Q R S T U V W X Y Z

Now write another helpful message in code.

Playground Fun

The playground is a place to have fun and play games safely.

Draw a plan of your playground.

Label what each place is for.

Using kind words

Think of all the nice things you can call someone. Unjumble the words to help you.

rdflinye

_____

levrce

_____

plteio

_____

elngte

_____

ephflul

_____

hpypa

_____

idnk

_____

neci

_____

atmsr

_____

odog

_____

Look here if you get stuck

smart   happy   helpful   kind   polite

clever   gentle   nice   friendly   good

Your name _____

Helper's name _____

Bin it!

Design a rubbish bin so fantastic that children would search the playground for litter to put in it.

Make it ...

colourful!

fun!

move!

talk!

Why do we need to put our rubbish in the bin?

- •
- •
- •

Your name _____

Helper's name _____

Clear up!

What is in the rubbish bins in your playground?

-
-
-
-

Draw a map of your playground and put crosses to show where the rubbish bins are.

L Pass the playground test

You have to pass a test to drive a car.

Write down what you need to learn to enjoy the playground.

L

L

L

L

Would you pass the playground test?

Why?

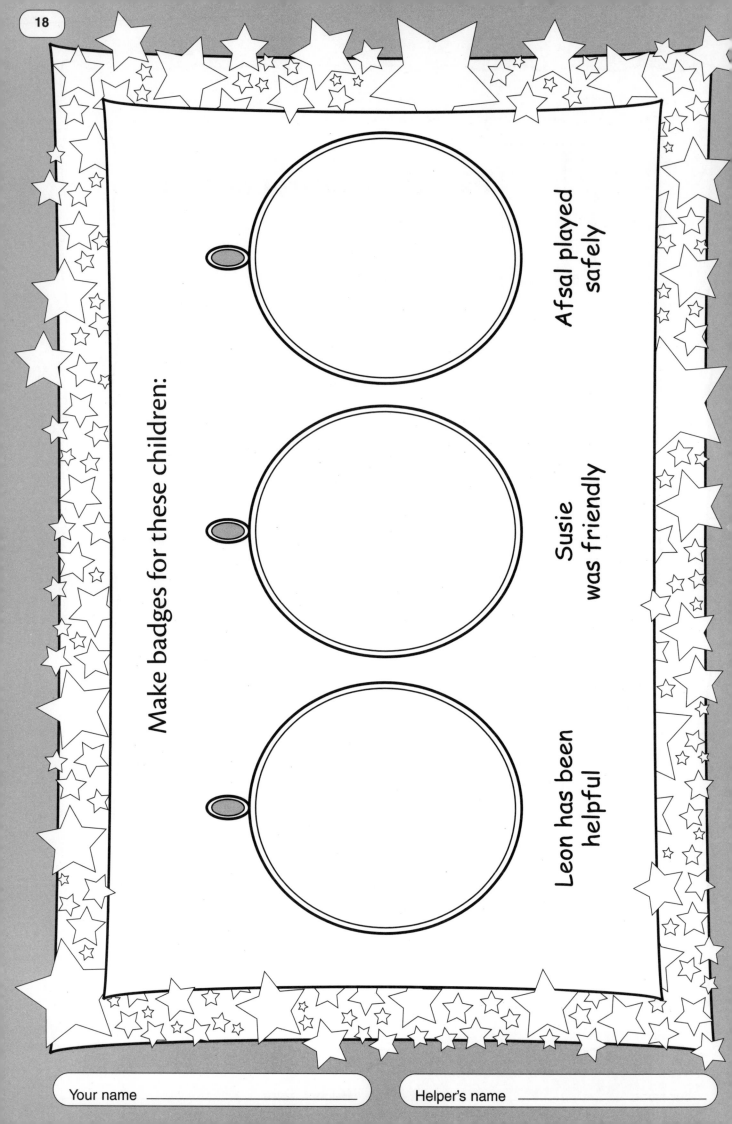

Make badges for these children:

Afsal played safely

Susie was friendly

Leon has been helpful

Your name _____

Helper's name _____

Making school a better place

Design a robot to pick up the litter in the playground.

Label all the working parts on your model.

How could this help everyone in your school?

Your name _____

Helper's name _____

Keeping the rules at lunchtime

You should not throw food – it is a waste.

Draw your favourite dinner.

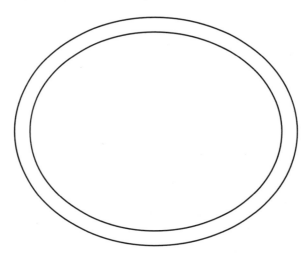

Think about lunchtime then finish the sentences.

When I have finished my meal:

- I put my tray ...

- I put my lunch box ...

- I ask to ...

- I go ...

Your name _____

Helper's name _____

Ball games

These are good games to play with a ball. Find the names of the games and write them under each ball. Choose from these games.

netball   **football**   **rugby**

uni-hoc   **rounders**   **cricket**   **tennis**

c k
i e t
r c

n s
n i t
e

n i u -
c o h

b g
r y
u

l a
l b n
t e

a l f l
o t o
b

n d u
e r s
o r

When can you play these games safely?

Where can you play these games safely?

My new game

The playground should be a place to have fun and play games. Invent a new playground game. Give it a name and write down how to play it.

Make a poster to remind all the children
about the playground rule:

We play safely in the playground
without..........

Your name _____   Helper's name _____

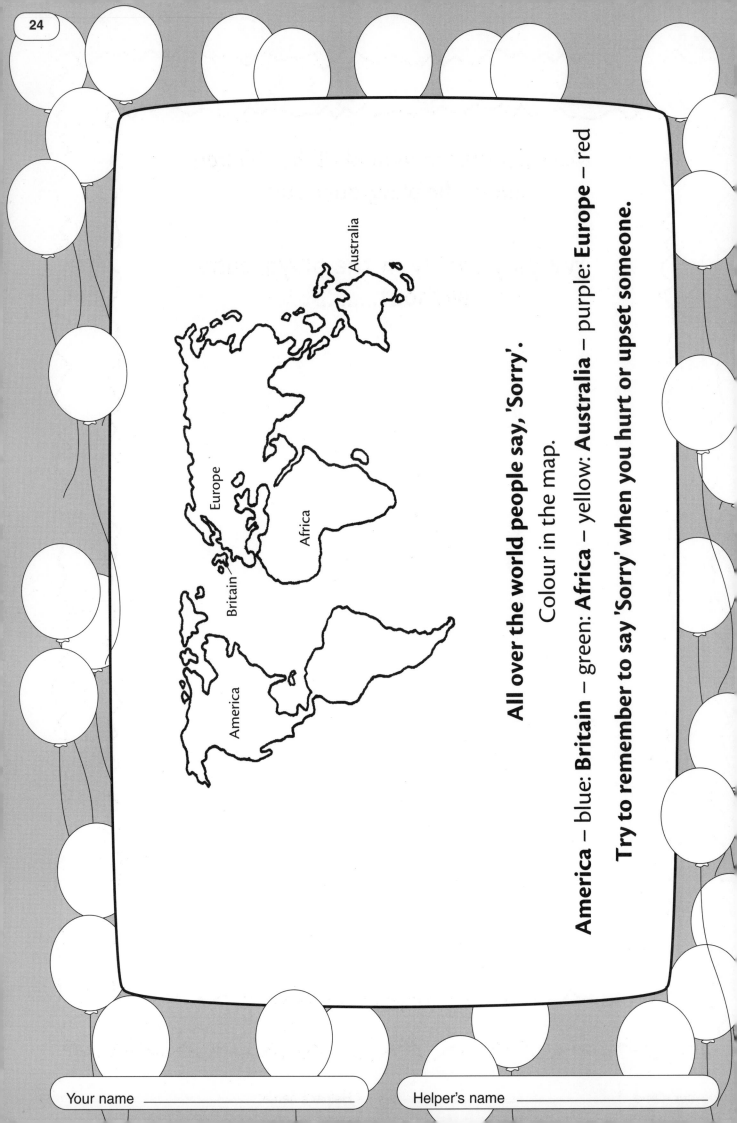

America – blue: **Britain** – green: **Africa** – yellow: **Australia** – purple: **Europe** – red

All over the world people say, 'Sorry'.
Colour in the map.

Try to remember to say 'Sorry' when you hurt or upset someone.

Australia

Europe

Africa

Britain

America

Your name _____

Helper's name _____

I should not play in the toilets because:

Draw

It is not safe.

Draw

I might fall and get hurt.

Your name _____

Helper's name _____

I should not play in the toilets because:

Draw

I might get dirty.

Draw

I might hurt someone.

Your name _____

Helper's name _____

If I take somebody else's things from a bag or a drawer, they will feel sad or angry

Draw an angry girl with long dark hair.
Make her clothes red and blue.

Draw a sad boy.
Make his clothes black and green.

Your name _____

Helper's name _____

We can use different real names and nicknames.

Nicknames can be friendly or hurtful.

Sort these names and think of some more for each list:

saddo   Ben   dummy   mate   Ann   thicko   cow   dear

star   love   plonker   Amir   idiot   pet   dog   Sally   creep

real names	friendly names	hurtful names

There are lots of good games to
play with one ball. Invent a new
game that you play with a football.

Write the rules.

Who would you
play this with?

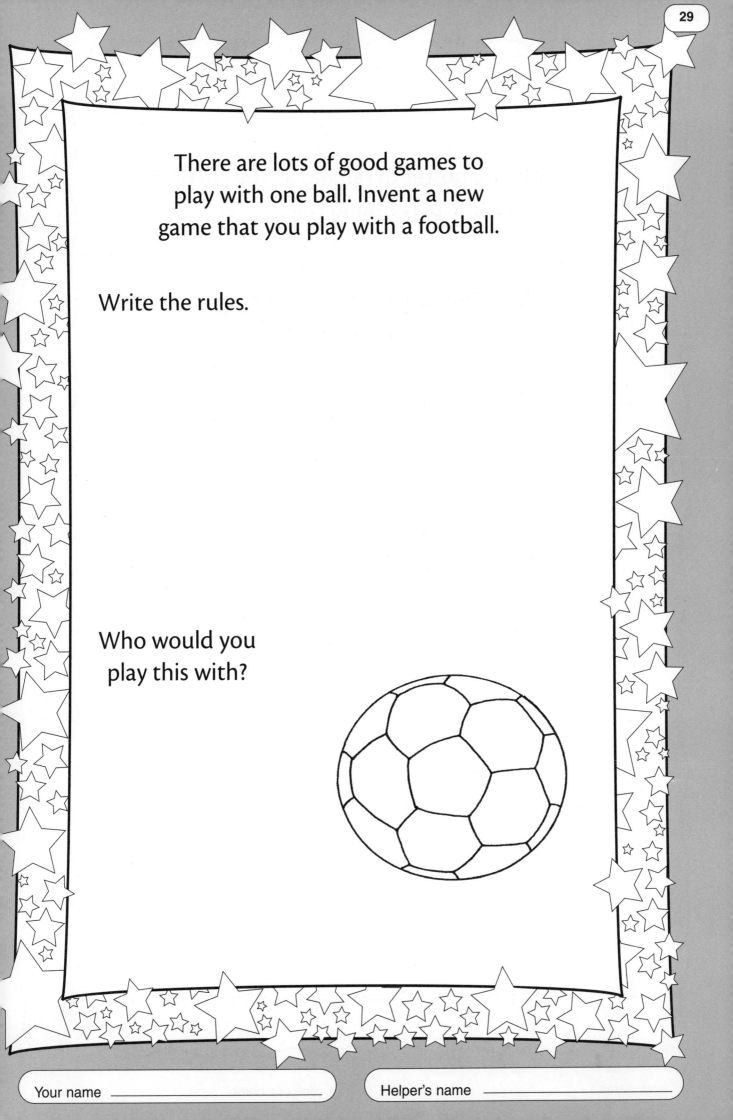

Your name _____   Helper's name _____

Make a poster to remind all the children about the playground rule:

We play safely in the playground without kicking.

Do not throw stones because:

Draw

You might break a window.

Draw

You might hurt someone.

Daily Newspaper

Child hurt climbing at school

Yesterday at a local school a child was badly hurt after climbing on ...

Some places are dangerous to climb.

Draw two of them

Some places are safe to climb.

Draw two of them

Your name _____   Helper's name _____

If you play on the grass ...

Draw

You might get muddy.

Draw

You might get wet shoes.

Your name _____

Helper's name _____

Moving safely

Colour the traffic lights red, amber and green.

Now write when you should:

Stop and stand still
·
·
·

Walk sensibly
·
·
·

Run around
·
·
·

Your name _____

Helper's name _____

It is dangerous to run in and out at play time.

Draw

You might fall over.

Draw

You might knock someone over.

Your name _____

Helper's name _____

Sharing information

Write a postcard to another school telling them about the good things children do in your playground.

Dear Friend

I am writing to tell you about the good things that happen in our playground

Love from

Design the front of your postcard to show children playing happily in the playground

Your name _____   Helper's name _____

The best things about playtime are:

Show four things that you like.

Never run in school

Draw four places where it is safe to run.

Keep out of trouble

Finish the acrostic to remind you how to behave in the playground.

It has been started for you.

Put your litter.........

Look.........

Always........

You must........

Go........

Running........

Only say........

Understand the rules.

Never........

Do not........

Understanding rules

People who keep to the rules are safe. They also have a good time. Take time to think about the rules for your playground.

Make a picture list of the games you **can** play.

Make a picture list of the games you **cannot** play.

Your name _____

Helper's name _____

Talk Kindly

We all like to be talked to kindly so we don't hurt others' feelings.

Think of better ways to say these things:

:(	:)
Go away, we don't want you to play with us.	
You're useless at football.	
Stop crying you baby.	
You're in trouble again you idiot.	
Can't you get to the top of the climbing frame you wimp?	

Your name _____

Helper's name _____

What other people think of me:

my friends

my teacher

the headteacher

my family

lunchtime helpers

Do you agree with these people?

Your name _____

Helper's name _____

My friends

Who do you play with?
Make the faces into your friends.

is a good friend
because

is a good friend
because

is a good friend
because

Your name _____

Helper's name _____

My friends

Who do you play with?

Make the faces into your friends.

gets me into
trouble because

gets me into
trouble because

gets me into
trouble because

Your name _____

Helper's name _____

Thinking about you

You are special. No one in the whole world is the same as you. You are the only one ... **You are unique.**

Draw your picture in the frame.

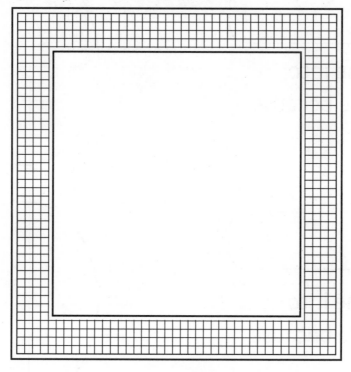

Circle the things that make you special:

kind   **strong**   **clever**

generous   **tough**

gentle   **happy**   **funny**   **nice**

quiet   **helpful**   **trustworthy**

loyal   **brave**   **witty**   **polite**

Your name _____   Helper's name _____

What do you do in the playground?

Put a tick in the right column.

	never	sometimes	a lot
play with bigger children			
feel sad			
sit quietly			
hate older children			
sit by yourself			
play with friends			
feel frightened			
stay by a grown-up			
run about			
play alone			
have fun			
feel angry			
play with girls			
play with boys			
use the Friendship Stop			
play with younger children			

Your name _____

Helper's name _____

48

Thinking about friends

Draw a picture of your best friend.

Name: _____

Age: _____

I like my friend because

_____

_____

_____

_____

Draw another friend.

They are a special friend because

Your name _____

Helper's name _____

Helping your friends

Draw your friend.

Name:

Age:

We are friends
because

I can help my friend stay out of trouble by:

• *helping him to keep calm*

•

•

•

•

Your name _____

Helper's name _____

Fill in the chart:

	playtime	lunchtime	after school
What do you do?			
Who do you play with?			
Who is on duty?			
What can you do?			
What can't you do?			
Do you like this time?			

Your name _____   Helper's name _____

Draw a map of the play spaces.

Colour the places you like to play.

I play here because:

Mark crosses at the places where you get into trouble.
I get into trouble here because ...

Your name _____

Helper's name _____

What do you do at lunchtime?

Do you have a school dinner or a packed lunch?
Use the right box and draw your favourite meal.
Label each food and your drink.

Packed lunch

School dinner

What should you do when it's time to go and have your dinner?

Your name _____   Helper's name _____

Understanding lunchtime rules

Fill in the chart to show what you must do.

	packed lunch	school dinner
I get my food ...		
I go ...		
My table is ...		
My coat goes ...		
I sit ...		
If I want a drink ...		
When I finish I ...		
I ask for help from ...		

Have you got any questions about what to do at lunchtime?

Your name _____   Helper's name _____

Feelings

Put a blue mark on the line to show how you feel when you get into trouble outside.

Sad   **Happy**

_____

Clever   **Silly**

_____

Embarrassed   **Proud**

_____

Pleased   **Angry**

_____

Big   **Small**

_____

Confident   **Scared**

_____

Now put a red mark on the line to show how you feel when you have behaved well.

Your name _____

Helper's name _____

Take time to think!

Why have you been sent in?

Use the boxes to show what happened.

What could you have done to stop it happening?

Your name _____

Helper's name _____

Information about friends

Friends are important. They are fun to be with, but sometimes we behave worse with our friends. They can be a 'bad influence'.

List your friends:

1 _____
2 _____
3 _____
4 _____
5 _____
6 _____
7 _____

Sort them into these boxes

Never in trouble

Often in trouble

Sometimes in trouble

Your name _____

Helper's name _____

Planning a good playtime

When does playtime start?

When does playtime finish?

It is _____ minutes long.

Draw what you do in the right order.

First ...	Then ...	Next ...	Lastly ...

Your name _____   Helper's name _____

Planning a good lunchtime

It starts at

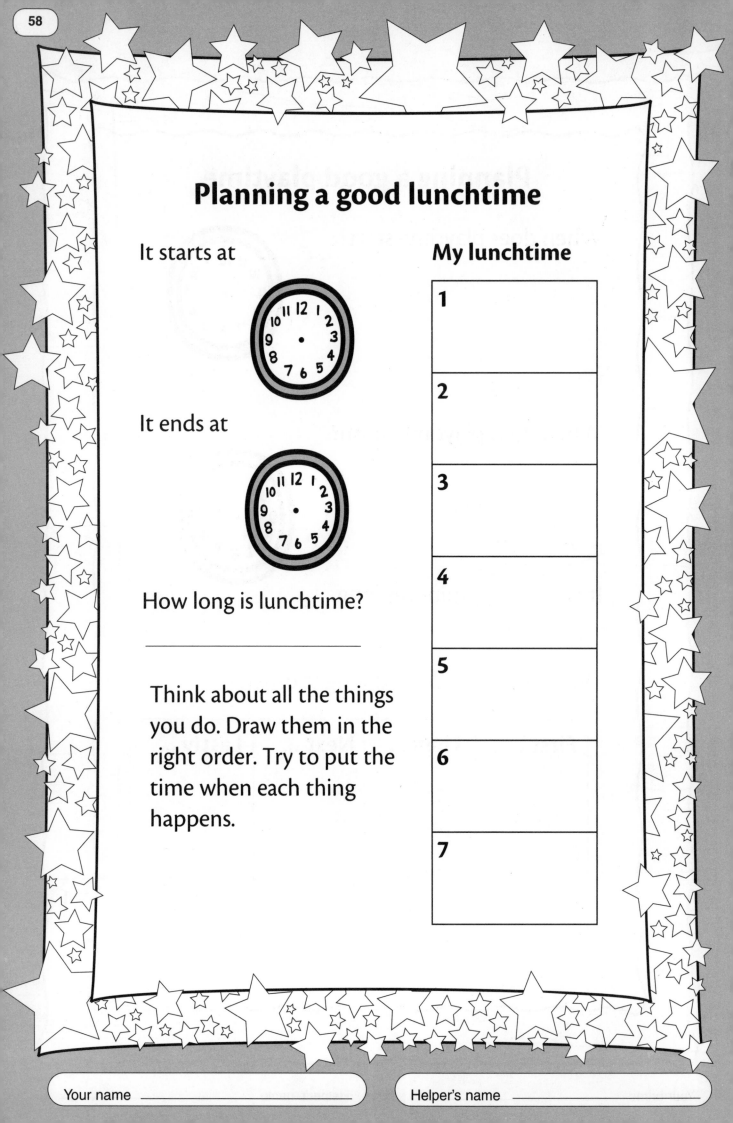

It ends at

How long is lunchtime?

_____

Think about all the things you do. Draw them in the right order. Try to put the time when each thing happens.

My lunchtime

1
2
3
4
5
6
7

Your name _____   Helper's name _____

Sort your friends into these sets:

fun to be with

sometimes nasty to me

Which friends should you play with?

Why?

Nobody is all bad!

Think of two people you do not like very much. Draw them.

Now think of three good things about the people you have drawn.

1.   1.

2.   2.

3.   3.

Your name _____   Helper's name _____

Do you know the rules?

People who understand the rules are:

- less likely to get into trouble
- more likely to have good friends
- more likely to have fun.

People who break the rules are:

- likely to get into trouble
- a danger to others
- less likely to enjoy themselves
- less likely to have friends.

Write down the rules you know for the playground.
Put a tick by the rules you keep.

1. ☐

2. ☐

3. ☐

4. ☐

5. ☐

Your name _____   Helper's name _____

If you were in charge ...

What would be **your** playground rules?

-
-
-

What **are** the playground rules?

What things are the same?

What things are different?

Your name _____   Helper's name _____

Keeping calm!

It's OK to feel:

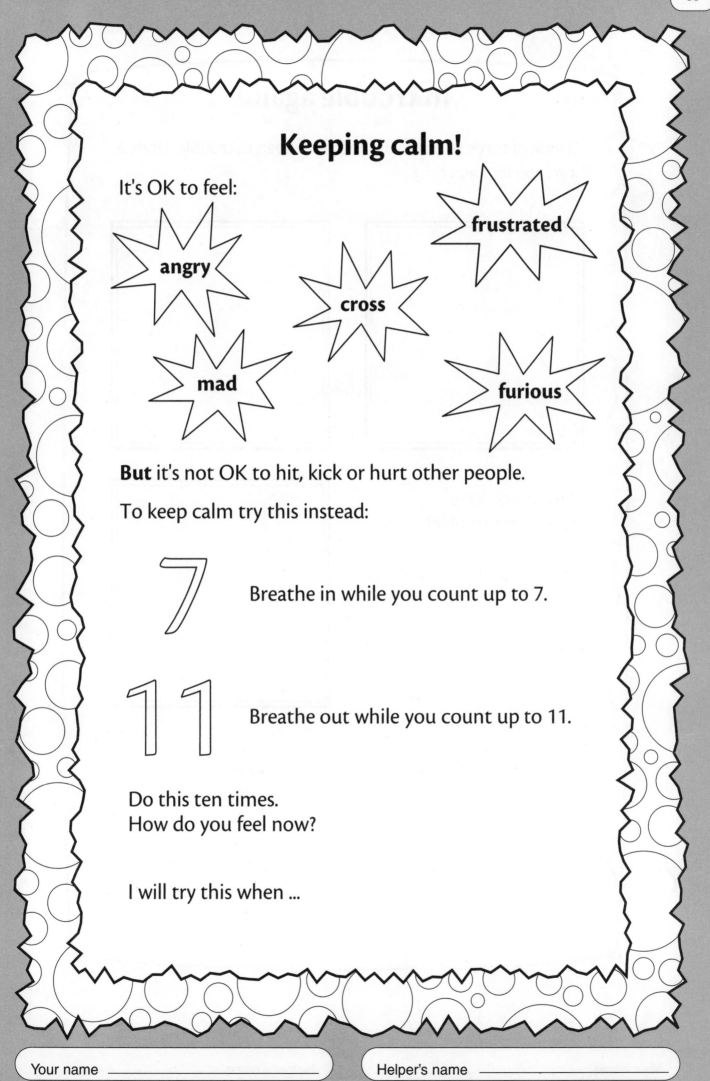

angry

frustrated

cross

mad

furious

But it's not OK to hit, kick or hurt other people.

To keep calm try this instead:

7   Breathe in while you count up to 7.

11   Breathe out while you count up to 11.

Do this ten times.
How do you feel now?

I will try this when ...

Your name _____ Helper's name _____

In trouble again!

Think of three reasons why you have been in trouble. Draw a cartoon for each time.

Why do you keep
getting into trouble?

What can you do to stop getting into trouble?

Your name _____

Helper's name _____

Choose four things you like doing in the playground. Put a ring round them.

singing   hiding   balancing

running   ball games

chasing   sitting   climbing

football   watching

jumping   talking

swinging   pretend games

shouting   skipping   resting

Do these things get you into trouble?

yes   no   sometimes

Write why.

Think about someone else

Draw your teacher.

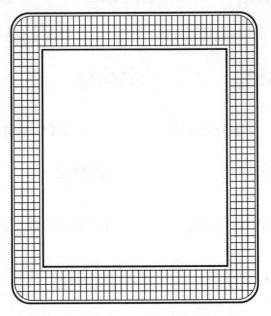

How does your teacher feel when you are in trouble?

What should your teacher say to you?

How will you put things right?

Your name _____

Helper's name _____

Think!

What would you do if ...

Someone knocked you over on purpose?

Someone knocked you over by accident?

Someone frightened you?

Someone said something rude about your family?

Are your ideas good or will they get you into trouble? Put a tick by all the good ideas and a cross by the bad ones.

Your name _____

Helper's name _____

Think!

How would you help if:

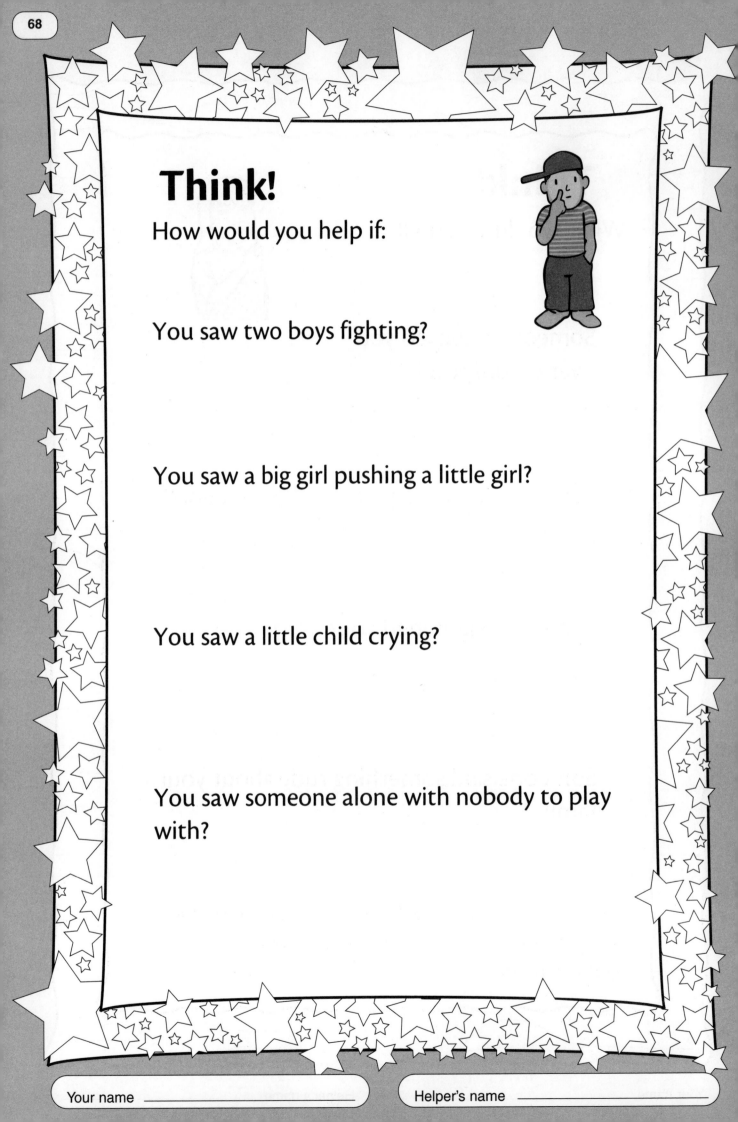

You saw two boys fighting?

You saw a big girl pushing a little girl?

You saw a little child crying?

You saw someone alone with nobody to play with?

Your name _____

Helper's name _____

Saying 'sorry'

'Sorry' is really important in any language

Colour all the words carefully.

Traurig
German

Pesaroso
Portugese

Désolé
French

Droevig
Dutch

Practise saying these and try them
on your friends.

Your name _____

Saying 'Sorry'

Sometimes saying 'Sorry' can be hard.

Take time to make a very special Sorry card to help you.

Think carefully about what to write inside.

Sorry

Please cut and fold

Your name _____   Helper's name _____

Helping others

These children need help.
How could you help them?
Draw the people and write what you would say.

I've fallen down.
My leg is cut.

Nobody will
play with me.

Your name _____

Helper's name _____

Helping someone else

These children need help.
How could you help them?
Draw the people and write what you would say.

> I can't find
> my coat.

> They keep calling
> me names.

Thinking about somebody else

Somebody has fallen over. Use the cartoon strip
to show what you could do to help.

Newcomers

A new child has come to your school who **hates** playtimes.

What could you do to help?

Share your ideas.

I would ...

Helping Ashley

Ashley is always in trouble.

Nobody will play with Ashley.

Ashley is fed up.

Ashley wants friends to play with.

Ashley needs help.

What do you suggest?

Your name _____   Helper's name _____

Making new friends

Here are some ideas for making new friends.

Draw the pictures to show what you would do.

I could tell someone a joke or do something to make them laugh.

I could share my snack at breaktime.

I could ask him or her to join in my game.

Your name _____

Helper's name _____

Wet play!

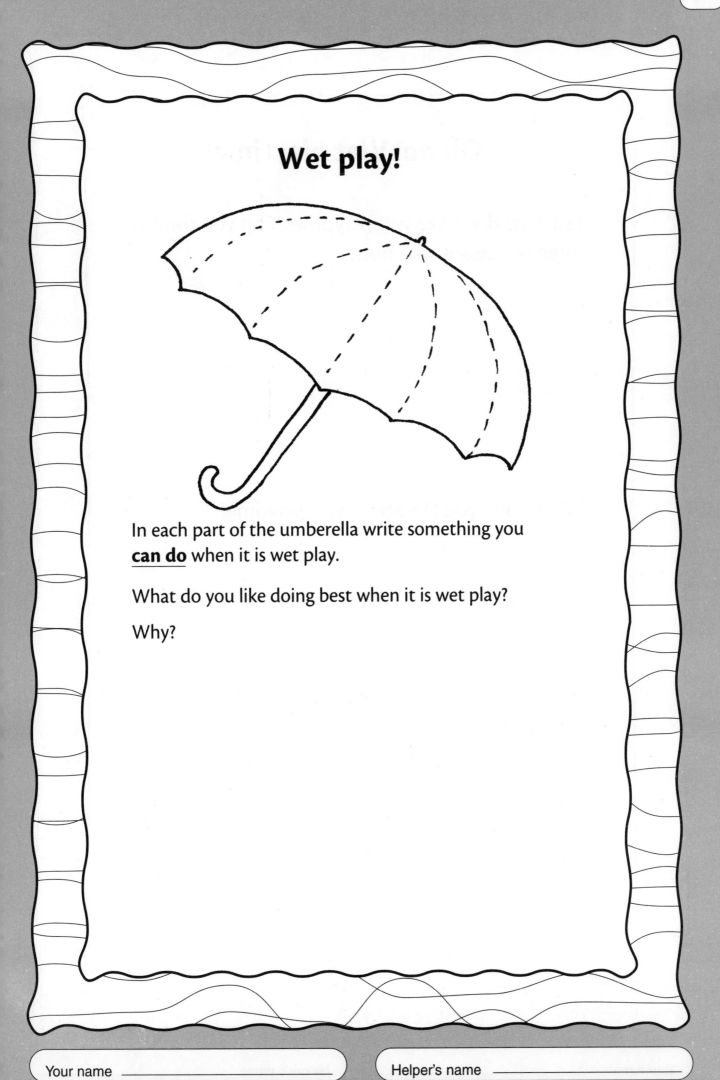

In each part of the umberella write something you **can do** when it is wet play.

What do you like doing best when it is wet play?

Why?

Your name _____   Helper's name _____

Oh no! Wet playtime!

Teachers don't like wet playtimes. Can you think of three of reasons why not?

1.

2.

3.

What don't you like about wet playtime?

How could wet playtimes be better? List your ideas:

-
-
-

Your name _____   Helper's name _____

Raining again

Circle in red the things you can do in the playground.

Circle in blue the things you can do when it is wet play.

Running   **Reading**   **Skipping**

Play board games   **Shouting**

Watch videos   **Drawing**

Play ball games

Write four things you can do at both kinds of playtime.

1.

2.

3.

4.

Your name _____   Helper's name _____

What you do matters

Think about the consequences if someone:

Problem	Consequence
threw your coat on the roof	
took your lunch box	
hid your sweatshirt	
threw your ball over the fence	
broke your toy	

What would you do next?

Your name _____

Helper's name _____

Your name _____

Helper's name _____

Your name _____   Helper's name _____

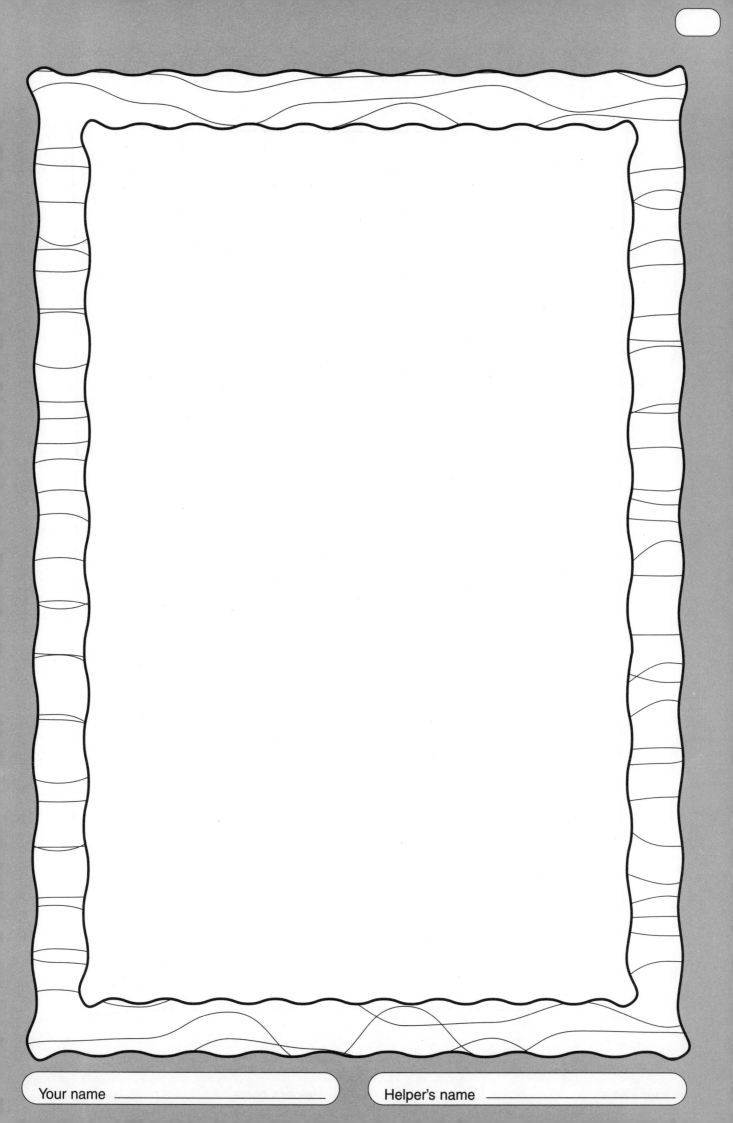

Your name _____

Helper's name _____

Your name _____

Helper's name _____

Your name _____   Helper's name _____

Your name _____

Helper's name _____

Your name _____   Helper's name _____

Your name _____   Helper's name _____